IMAGES
of America

THE
JEKYLL ISLAND
CLUB

This book is dedicated to my parents, Charles and Susan, and to J. Wesley Wellman. (JIM.)

IMAGES
of America

THE
JEKYLL ISLAND
CLUB

Tyler E. Bagwell
Jekyll Island Museum

ARCADIA

Copyright © 1998 by Tyler E. Bagwell and the Jekyll Island Museum.
ISBN 0-7524-0935-2

First published 1998.
Reprinted 1999, 2000, 2001, 2002, 2003.

Published by Arcadia Publishing,
an imprint of Tempus Publishing, Inc.
2 Cumberland Street
Charleston, SC 29401

Printed in Great Britain.

For all general information contact Arcadia Publishing at:
Telephone 843-853-2070
Fax 843-853-0044
E-Mail sales@arcadiapublishing.com

For customer service and orders:
Toll-Free 1-888-313-2665

Visit us on the internet at http://www.arcadiapublishing.com

"The real core of life in Jekyl Island's great days was to be found in the men's after-dinner talks. It was always of great things, of visions and developing. If they didn't have a map of the United States or the World before them, they had a map of industrial or financial empires in their minds."—Quote attributed by Nancy Albright Hurd to Dr. Walter Belknap James, photograph c. early 1900s. (JIM.)

CONTENTS

INTRODUCTION

It was an elite club, one impossible for most socialites to join. Its roster was restricted to only 100 members, and boasted economic leaders and prominent American families. Some of the notables on the membership list included Pierre Lorillard, Marshall Field, J.P. Morgan, William Rockefeller, and William Vanderbilt. The club stressed simplicity, and in contrast to other clubs for the wealthy, it certainly was simple. They named it the Jekyll Island Club.

For decades, Jekyll Island was owned by the du Bignon family, who cultivated cotton on large portions of the island's acreage. However, the loss of slave labor ended the island's plantation era. In 1886, the patriarch of the du Bignon family's great-grandson, John Eugene du Bignon, along with the assistance of his business-savvy brother-in-law, Newton Finney, sold the island to an incorporated hunting and recreational club for $125,000. In the beginning, most of the Jekyll Island Club members were connected by their association with the prestigious New York Union Club, of which Newton Finney and his business partner Oliver King were members. The respected King, secretary of the New York Union Club, influenced many wealthy industrialists into joining the club sight unseen.

Virtually unspoiled by development, Jekyll Island's sub-tropical weather created an ideal geographic area for a winter resort. The surrounding Atlantic waters provided a prime location for catching seafood such as shrimp and oysters. Virginal beaches expanded at low tide, forming hard-packed sand thoroughfares perfect for moonlit horse and carriage rides. The island interior, consisting of Spanish moss-draped forest and fallow cotton fields, was habitat for deer, turkeys, raccoons, and song birds. Scattered ponds housed wild ducks and toothy alligators.

By 1888, a clubhouse was constructed and ready for occupancy. Eventually, some of the members built mansion-size cottages and all but one were located within walking distance of the clubhouse. In the early years, hunting was a favorite activity, but in time, other sports, such as golf, lawn bowling, and tennis became popular. Evenings were spent in the clubhouse dining on elaborate multi-course meals. Afterwards, members and guest enjoyed billiards, cards, dancing, or fireside chats.

Besides owning a share in the club, members were required to pay annual dues. In 1888, dues were $100, but by 1933, they had risen to $700. Members also paid for staying in bedrooms, dining, and using club amenities such as carriages. In times of income deficits or renovations of club structures, funding subscriptions were obtained from the members. Some accepted a greater responsibility in financing the club than others. For example, in 1918 J.P. Morgan Jr. donated $10,000 towards the debt the club had incurred while enlarging the dining room and adding more bedrooms to the clubhouse.

At its height of popularity, the club resembled a village-like compound. Close to being self-sufficient, the chefs of the club utilized the island's vegetable gardens, dairy, oyster beds, and terrapin pens. Electricity was furnished by a power plant and artesian wells supplied the water. A doctor was present almost every club season, and in later years, an infirmary, or hospital, was added.

Over the club's 54-year span, several unique events took place. In 1899, the club boasted a visit by President William McKinley. In 1910, a secret island meeting was held in which the Federal Reserve System was initiated. In 1915, the club participated in the first telephone call across the United States. A yellow fever outbreak in 1894 officially canceled the season, although some still braved the danger to visit. A hurricane devastated the island in 1898, eroding the beach and destroying the wharf and island bridges. A typhoid fever epidemic resulted in the death of a member's wife in 1909.

Major membership changes occurred in the 1910s. Aging members such as James J. Hill, Joseph Pulitzer, and J.P. Morgan died during this decade. While some joining the club were spouses or children of former members, such as James J. Hill's wife Mary and J.P. Morgan Jr., many were new recruits, such as Vincent Astor, Richard T. Crane, and Theodore Vail.

The 1920s were a prosperous time for the club, and amenities such as the "Red Bugs," a swimming pool, and an upgraded golf course were added. As had happened in the 1910s, membership changes were taking place. More longtime members died, including Charles Maurice and William Rockefeller. More children of members joined, and more new members were recruited, such as Walter Jennings and Bernon Prentice.

The last vestiges of the club's old guard, longtime members such as John J. Albright, George Baker, and John Claflin, died in the 1930s. In addition, besides the fact that by this time Victorian-style architecture was no longer in vogue, the stock market crash of 1929 plunged the country into economic turmoil and the club into a dilemma, as many of the members were resigning due to financial hardships. To combat this problem, in 1933, members owning a share in the club were reclassified as founders and a new type of membership, called an associate membership, was created. Associate members, whose numbers were limited to 150, enjoyed island amenities like the founders did, but their annual dues were less expensive.

In late 1941, with the bombing of Pearl Harbor, the United States was pulled into World War II. The club remained open for the 1942 season, but after closing at the end of the season, it would never re-open. By the summer of 1942, many of the club employees as well as some of the members were drafted into the military, and because of rationing, food, fuel, and supplies were difficult to obtain for the club. Plans to open for the 1943 season were canceled.

From 1942 to at least 1946, the club maintained a small staff of employees on the island and received lawn care assistance from the Sea Island Company. During WW II, several branches of the military were based on the island, including the Coast Guard, Army, and Navy. The Army resided in the club's boardinghouse, and the Navy lived in the tea house. Also, in 1943 the Georgia National Guard, while staying in the servants' annex, participated in a training session.

In 1947, through condemnation proceedings, the state of Georgia bought the island from the remaining club members for $675,000. The purchase gave the public access to Jekyll's beaches. For some the island sale was a relief, as taxes were mounting and the only source of revenue for the club was an island timber-cutting contract. For others, the sale was a disappointment. Some members desired to revamp the club and construct a bridge to the island. Nevertheless, the sale still took place, and included the entire island, the structures, and some furnishings.

In 1979 the island area containing the clubhouse and cottages was designated a National Historic Landmark district by the Department of the Interior. Currently, the island is maintained by the Jekyll Island Authority, a self-sufficient entity created by the state of Georgia. The Jekyll Island Museum, an Authority division, is preserving the historic district for present and future generations.

Here are a few tips for understanding the book's layout. Within parentheses following the text for each photograph is the name of where the image was obtained; however, if the image is from the Jekyll Island Museum, the name has been abbreviated JIM. Membership dates are given within parentheses following the names of members. If a member is mentioned more than once, the dates are omitted after the first acknowledgment. If the person was an associate member, his designation is abbreviated A.M.

Readers will notice that in several pictures taken before 1929 the name "Jekyll" appears as "Jekyl." An example can be seen on page 24 on the side of the club's steamer. During English colonization, the island was named after Sir Joseph Jekyll, a Georgia colony financial backer. However, for unknown reasons the final letter of his name was deleted in the late 1700s. Through correspondence with a Jekyll family descendant, then-club President Walter Jennings discovered that the name was misspelled. With encouragement from club members, the 1929 legislature passed a resolution correcting the spelling mistake in legal and state documents. The contemporary spelling of "Jekyll" is used throughout the book except in the case of a book title and the club's passenger boat.

Presidents of the Jekyll Island Club

1. Lloyd Aspinwall   1886–1887
2. Henry Howland   1887–1896
3. Charles Lanier   1897–1914
4. Frederick Bourne   1914–1919
5. Dr. Walter James   1919–1927
6. Walter Jennings   1927–1933
7. J.P. Morgan Jr.   1933–1938
8. Bernon Prentice   1938–1942

Emblems of the Jekyll Island Club

1890s–1920s

Early 1900s, used on dining accoutrements

1930s–1940s

One

CLUBHOUSE, COTTAGES, AND MEMBERS

"Its purpose shall be to own and maintain a hunting, fishing, yachting, and general sporting resort, to promote social intercourse among its members and their families, and to carry out such other purpose authorized by its charter as may be determined by the Board of Directors." Jekyl Island Club Officers, members, Constitution, Bylaws and Charter book, c. 1902. (Courtesy of the Coastal Georgia Historical Society.)

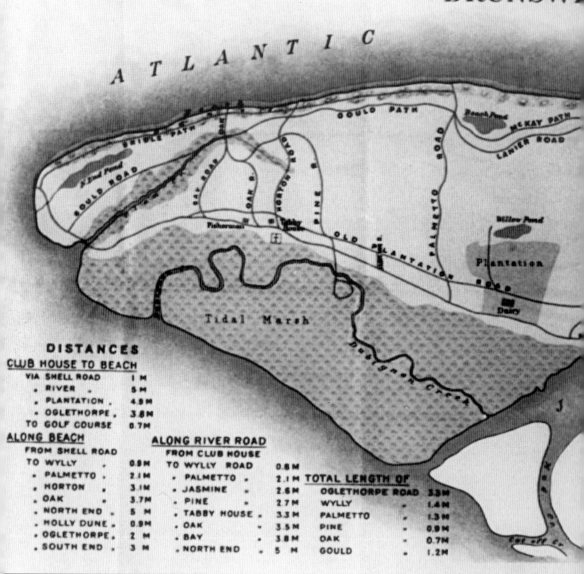

ATLANTIC

GOULD PATH

Beach Pond

McKAY PATH

LANIER ROAD

ROAD

BRIDLE PATH

GOULD ROAD

N. End Pond

OAK

BAY ROAD

OLD ROAD

HORTON ROAD

PINE

PALMETTO

Willow Pond

Fisherman

OLD PLANTATION

Plantation

ROAD

Tidal Marsh

Dairy

Raccoon Creek

J

DISTANCES

CLUB HOUSE TO BEACH

VIA SHELL ROAD		1 M
" RIVER "		5 M
" PLANTATION "		4.9 M
" OGLETHORPE "		3.8 M
TO GOLF COURSE		0.7 M

ALONG BEACH

FROM SHELL ROAD		
TO WYLLY	"	0.9 M
" PALMETTO "		2.1 M
" HORTON "		3.1 M
" OAK "		3.7 M
" NORTH END "		5 M
" MOLLY DUNE "		0.9 M
" OGLETHORPE "		2 M
" SOUTH END "		3 M

ALONG RIVER ROAD

FROM CLUB HOUSE		
TO WYLLY ROAD		0.8 M
" PALMETTO "		2.1 M
" JASMINE "		2.6 M
" PINE "		2.7 M
" TABBY HOUSE "		3.3 M
" OAK "		3.5 M
" BAY "		3.8 M
" NORTH END "		5 M

TOTAL LENGTH OF

OGLETHORPE ROAD		3.5 M
WYLLY	"	1.4 M
PALMETTO	"	1.3 M
PINE	"	0.9 M
OAK	"	0.7 M
GOULD	"	1.2 M

This picture is dated *c.* 1920s. The club called the region of the island where the clubhouse and cottages were located the enclosure or compound. To keep wild animals out of the area, a fence encircled the enclosure. With the exception of Horton, Old Plantation, and Wylly, all of the island roads were constructed by the club. Horton Road was established during English colonization by Major William Horton, who initially needed sand from the dunes to construct

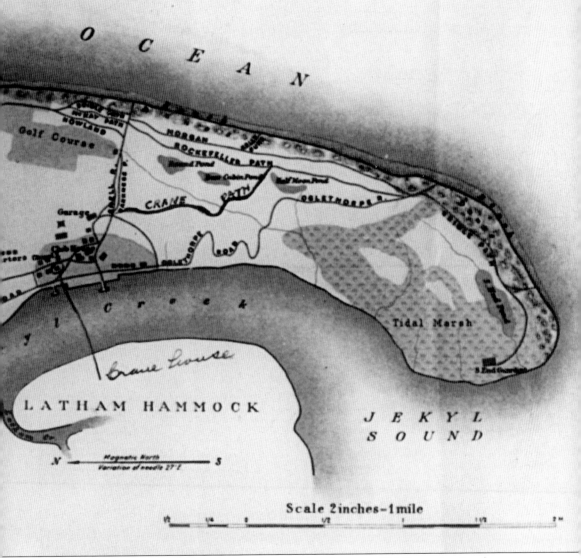

OCEAN

Golf Course

MORGAN

ROCKEFELLER PATH

CRANE PATH

OGLETHORPE R.

OGLETHORPE ROAD

Garage

C r e e k

Tidal Marsh

S. End Coast Guard

Crane House

LATHAM HAMMOCK

JEKYL
SOUND

N — Magnetic North — S
Variation of needle 27° E

Scale 2 inches–1 mile

his tabby buildings. The road later became his main beach access. Old Plantation Road was one of the primary north-south routes used during the island's agricultural period. The third road, Wylly, was built in the early 1800s by Capt. Alexander Wylly, who cultivated cotton on a large section of leased land. (JIM.)

Marshall Field (m. 1886–1906), a founding member, was the head of Marshall Field & Company, a dry goods store, as well as the owner of large real estate tracts in Chicago's business district. His brother, Henry Field (m. 1886–90), also belonged to the club. Many of the members were related either through business dealings or family relationships. (JIM.)

Another founding member, John Pierpont Morgan (m. 1886–1913), was in charge of the J.P. Morgan & Company. Essentially an investment banker, he was well known for reorganizing and consolidating existing companies. Mr. Morgan had several cohorts affiliated with the club, including his brother-in-law, Alfred Pell (m. 1898–1901), and business partners Samuel Spencer (m. 1898–1906), Henry P. Davison (m. 1912–17, A.M.), and Edward Stotesbury (m. 1909–19). (Courtesy of the Pierpont Morgan Library.)

The J.P. Morgan & Company, by
consolidating several farming
equipment businesses, including
McCormick Harvesting Company and
Deering Company, in 1902 created the
International Harvester Company.
Cyrus Hall McCormick Jr.
(m. 1891–1936), seen right, became
president of the International
Harvester Company and another
member, Charles Deering
(m. 1887–1902), became chair of the
board of directors. (JIM.)

George F. Baker (m. 1901–31), seen
left, was president of the First National
Bank. His brother-in-law, Grant B.
Schley (m. 1903–17), his grandson,
George Baker St. George (m. 1926–28),
as well as his personal physician, Dr.
George Stewart (m. 1925–33) were all
members. (JIM.)

The picture above is c. 1890; the picture below is c. 1930s. Most of the club members resided in the clubhouse, a hotel-like structure. The first floor of the clubhouse consisted of an office, lobby, dining room, and five other chambers. In 1897, a billiards room was added by an extension to the clubhouse. Located on the first floor toward the end of the club period was a library, furnished with lounge chairs and a large selection of books, as well as a smoking room, with a leather sofa and mahogany-framed leather chairs. A card room was equipped with oak and green felt card tables and numerous bentwood and cane chairs. The parlor was decorated with love seats, lounge chairs, and an oil portrait of the island's namesake, Sir Joseph Jekyll. The second, third, and fourth floors consisted of bedrooms. (both JIM.)

In the background of this c. 1893 picture (far left) a bulletin board and the office check-in window are seen from the clubhouse lobby. The bulletin board displayed a list of members delinquent in their dues, and, since newspapers were days old upon arrival, it also included a telegraph of the recent news events. In the early years, the hunting rules as well as approximate location of persons out shooting with rifles were posted. (JIM.)

In later years, the parlor (seen above), c. 1890s, was turned into a library. To insure impartiality, the club did not allow members to reserve rooms in advance. Instead, members selected from the vacant rooms available upon arrival. In 1900, a room for two with a bathroom cost $13.50 a day. By 1941, the same type of room ranged from $28 to $32 a day. (JIM.)

While checking-in, members were designated a table in the dining room where, for dinners, the protocol of formal dress was expected. Meals were multi-course and often included locally caught cuisine such as Jekyl Oysters on the Half Shell, Stuffed Crab Ravigotte, and Shrimp Salad. The dining room was remodeled in 1896 and enlarged by a semi-circle addition, seen above. In 1917, the dining room (seen below), *c.* 1937, was extended into a large rectangular shape. (both JIM.)

The picture above is dated c. 1920s; the one below is c. 1903. Angling from the clubhouse billiards room, eight private apartments and 20 additional bedrooms were constructed in 1901. Throughout the club period, with the exception of the Spencer family apartment, each one was owned by several different members and their families. The first apartment owners were John S. Kennedy (m. 1898–1909), a retired banker; Cornelius Bliss (m. 1886–1911), former secretary of the interior, as well as a partner in Bliss, Fabyan, & Company, a dry goods distributing firm; John J. Albright (m. 1890–1931), a coal industrialist; Charles Lanier (m. 1889–1926), a banker in Winslow, Lanier, & Company; Francis Bartlett (m. 1886–1911), a lawyer; Morris K. Jesup (m. 1888–1908), a railroad supplier and a partner with John S. Kennedy in Jesup, Kennedy, & Company; Edmund Hayes (m. 1886–1921), a civil engineer; and Samuel Spencer, president of the Southern Railroad Company and a J.P. Morgan & Company partner. (both JIM.)

In November of 1910, under the subterfuge of a duck-shooting excursion, a group of financial experts held a secret conference on Jekyll Island. The hunt in reality was for a way to restructure America's banking system and eliminate economic crises such as the banking panic of 1907. Congress formed the National Monetary Commission to review American banking policies. The committee, chaired by Sen. Nelson W. Aldrich (m.1912–1915) of Rhode Island, toured Europe and collected banking data. Using this information, Senator Aldrich, seen in the early 1900s at left, held a 10-day conference on Jekyll with several bankers and economic scholars. The group solution called for the creation of a central bank. (JIM.)

The 1910 banking reform conference on Jekyll included Senator Aldrich, his personal secretary Mr. Shelton, Dr. A. Piatt Andrew, Henry P. Davison, Frank A. Vanderlip, and Paul M. Warburg. Frank Vanderlip, president of National City Bank, is seen above in the early 1900s. The group met in secret and shunned the use of their last names throughout the trip. B.C. Forbes wrote of the Jekyll conference in his 1916 book *Men Who Are Making America*, "To this day these financiers are Frank and Harry and Paul [and Piatt] to one another and the late Senator remained 'Nelson' to them until his death. Later Benjamin Strong, Jr., was called into frequent consultation and he joined the 'First-Name Club' as 'Ben.'"(JIM.)

A letter written by Paul Warburg, published in *Henry P. Davison: The Record of a Useful Life*, offered an account of the 1910 conference. He recalled, "After we had completed the sketch of the bill, and before setting down to its definitive formulation, it was decided that we had earned 'a day off' which was to be devoted to duck shooting." Warburg, a partner in the banking firm Kuhn, Loeb, & Co., is pictured above at left *c.* early 1900s. Above at right, Henry Davison, a J.P. Morgan & Co. partner, is viewed *c.* 1910s. By 1912 both Aldrich and Davison were members of the Jekyll Island Club. (both JIM.)

Dr. A. Piatt Andrew is seen at right *c.* early 1900s. In 1910 Dr. Andrew, a former economics professor at Harvard University, was the Assistant Secretary to the Treasury. The National Monetary Commission appointed Piatt Andrew as one of their advisors and placed him in charge of editing the committee's publications. Although Congress did not pass the banking reform proposal submitted by Senator Aldrich, it did approve a similar plan in 1913 called the Federal Reserve Act. (JIM.)

On January 25, 1915, Theodore Vail (m. 1912–20), president of AT&T, participated, from Jekyll, in the ceremonial opening of the first transcontinental telephone line. A leg injury forced Mr. Vail to stay on the island instead of traveling to New York for the event. The ceremony, a four-way call, began with telephone inventor Alexander Graham Bell speaking from New York to his assistant, Thomas Watson, in San Francisco. Mr. Vail and others listened keenly in the clubhouse. A short time later, Pres. Woodrow Wilson congratulated everyone from a phone in Washington, D.C. Seen above, Theodore Vail holds a telephone as William Rockefeller (m. 1886–1922) listens to the conversation. Standing, c. 1915, from left to right, are Welles Bosworth, architect of the AT&T main office; Samuel B.P. Trowbridge, architect of the J.P. Morgan & Company building; and J.P. Morgan Jr. (m. 1913–1943). (JIM.)

The clubhouse, as the heart of the association, pulsated with activity every season. Above, *c.* 1899, two cousins, Duncan Steuart Ellsworth (m. 1895–1908), second from left, and John Magee (m. 1893–1908), far right, socialize with companions. Both members inherited income from coal-mining operations and railroad interests in New York. (JIM.)

J.P. Morgan Jr., standing left in this *c.* 1938 picture, became a member after the death of his father. His sons, Henry (A.M.) and Junius (A.M.), his cousin Ellen, who married William Vaughn (m. 1928–41), as well as his business partners, George Whitney (m. 1928–41), Francis Bartow (m. 1931–45), and Thomas Lamont (A.M.) were all members of the club. Standing right, Bernon Prentice (m. 1924–47), a partner in the company of Dominick & Dominick, became a member through his father-in-law, James Ellsworth (m. 1915–24), a banker. Mr. Prentice's brother-in-law, Reeve Schley (A.M.), also a banker, joined the club as well. (JIM.)

Members and guests arrived and departed the island by boat. Above, from left to right, Charles Stewart Maurice (m. 1886–1924), J.P. Morgan, and John Claflin (m. 1886–1912, 1921–38) converse at the club dock. Below, c. 1916, the wharf is viewed soon after its 1916 renovation. (both JIM.)

A boat departs the wharf (seen right) c. 1899, for Brunswick. In 1941, trunks were transported round trip from Brunswick at 50¢ each and hand baggage at 25¢ each. (JIM.)

While most of the members traveled to Brunswick by train and proceeded to the island by the club's private steamboat, some chose to sail down the Atlantic in a private yacht. Many of the yachts, like floating mansions, were too gigantic for the club dock and, thus, upon arrival, anchored off the north end of the island. Pictured above, c. 1910, a ship, possibly delivering coal, overshadows the wharf. (JIM.)

In 1901, the club purchased the steamer *Jekyl Island*, shown in the *c.* 1928–29 picture to the left, to replace the *Howland*, a boat named after Judge Henry Howland (m. 1886–1901). During the summer, the *Jekyl Island* was stored in the boathouse, and the *Hattie*, a smaller steamer named after a term for a horse or mule hitching rack, became the main transport. (JIM.)

Seen above, the *Kitty*, a steam launch named after Charles Lanier's niece, was built to replace the *Hattie*. By the late 1910s, the *Kitty* was replaced by the quicker *Sylvia*, a gasoline boat possibly named after the daughter of Robert Brewster (m. 1912–39), a Standard Oil Company executive. In the mid 1930s, the *Sydney*, a gasoline-powered launch using two engines, was purchased. The club also owned several small Naphtha launches and used them for local excursions and fishing expeditions. (JIM.)

A home built in 1884 by John Eugene du Bignon (m. 1886–96) was furnished by the club and offered to members on a rental basis. Called the Club Cottage, in 1899 the structure rented for $15 a day, however, if rented for over two months the price was reduced to $10 a day. In the *c.* 1915 picture below, a road sign near the Club Cottage states, "Automobiles are restricted to 6 miles per hour on all roads except the beach." Seen at right, bicyclers pause for a break in front of the Club Cottage, *c.* 1899. (both JIM.)

The picture here is dated *c.* 1920s. In 1888, the quirky banker, McEvers Bayard Brown (m.1886–1926), received the distinction of being the first member to construct a cottage, but, oddly, he most likely never visited the island! A legend claims that Mr. Brown lost interest in the United States after a romance left him broken-hearted. From the 1890s to his death in 1926, he lived on board his yacht in a small English port located off the Essex coast. Even stranger, he continued to pay his club dues and also financed maintenance to his cottage. His cousins, William Bayard Cutting (m. 1886–1912) and Robert Fulton Cutting (m. 1923–34) apparently lost contact with their hermit-like relative when he left America. In 1900, Brown's island home was offered as a completely furnished rental cottage for $200 a month. There were probably few, if any, renters due to the distant location of the cottage to the club enclosure. Ultimately, the structure became the residence of club employees, including James Clark, the boat captain, and John F. Courier, a boat engineer. (JIM.)

In 1890, Nathaniel Kellogg Fairbank (m. 1886–1903), an oil and lard refiner, erected a cottage on prime ground near the clubhouse. A few years after Fairbank's death, Walton Ferguson (m. 1887–1922) bought the home. Mr. Ferguson, besides being a director in the Union Carbide Company, was a banker in the firm of J & S Ferguson. His son Walton Jr. (m. 1902–06) also joined the club. (JIM.)

Ralph Strassburger (m. 1919–24) purchased the Fairbank cottage by the early 1920s. His wife, Mae, was the daughter of Frederick G. Bourne (m. 1901–19), president of the Singer Sewing Machine Company. By the late 1920s, Mrs. Strassburger's sister, Marjorie Bourne (m. 1920–29), and her husband, Alexander Thayer (m. 1929–37), owned the cottage. Another of Frederick Bourne's daughters, Marion (m. 1919–37), and her husband, Robert Elbert (m. 1926–29), were also club members. (JIM.)

Charles Stewart Maurice (m. 1886–1924), a civil engineer, constructed a cottage in 1890 using tabby as the principle building material. This picture is c. 1890s. Tabby, a concoction of crushed oyster shells, sand, lime, and water, was incorporated by the English during colonization of the southern coastal region. (JIM.)

Besides having a facade of historical significance, this cottage, c. 1890s, named Hollybourne, used bridge design features in its architecture. For example, trusses, similar to those used on railroad bridges, supported a section of the second-level floor, thereby, eliminating bearing walls in two of the first-floor rooms. (JIM.)

Charles Stewart Maurice, seen right, was a partner in the Union Bridge Building Company, which, during the 1880s, was the largest bridge construction firm in the world. Thomas Clark (m. 1886–96), Edmund Hayes, and George Spencer Field (m. 1891–97) were also partners in the company. After the death of Mr. Maurice, his son Archibald (m. 1924–28) and his daughter Margaret (m. 1924–47) joined the club. (JIM.)

Mr. Maurice's wife, Charlotte, seen left, contracted typhoid fever in 1909 while vacationing on Jekyll. She died from the disease later that year. It wasn't until 1912 that a possible cause for her illness was determined. Raw oysters were being harvested and stored near the sewage discharge line. To help prevent future outbreaks, the club constructed better sewage disposal facilities. The Maurices were knowledgeable on the coastal history, and, in 1926, their daughter Margaret published stories collected by Mrs. Maurice on the history and legends of Jekyll Island. Included in the short booklet was an article by Mr. Maurice on the club's early years. (JIM.)

True to Victorian decor, Hollybourne cottage had stuffed birds arranged on the fireplace mantel, and its hallway's oak floors were adorned with an animal skin rug in this c. 1890s picture. Predominantly displayed next to the fireplace was a spinning wheel. It was possibly a hobby, but more likely an ornamental object representing the Maurices appreciation for history. (JIM.)

The parlor shown above, c. 1890s, was decorated with hardwood and wicker furniture. Paintings hung from picture molding, avoiding damage to the plaster walls. The french doors led to a porch where, on occasion, the Maurices enjoyed tea. (JIM)

The above picture is dated c. 1903. Eighteen ninety was a bustling year for cottage construction, and Frederic Baker (m. 1888–1913) and his wife, Frances (m. 1897–1905, 1913–19), kept the trend active. Mr. Baker was a partner in Baker & Williams, a warehouse storage company. His stepson, Henry Lake (m. 1912–17), was also a member. During March of 1899, their cottage, named Solterra, was the focal point of island excitement. President McKinley, at the invitation of Cornelius Bliss, stayed at the Baker's home during a brief visit. Simultaneously, the Speaker of the House, Thomas Reed, vacationed as the guest of John G. Moore (m. 1892–99), a stockbroker. Soon after the death of Frederic Baker, tragedy struck Solterra Cottage (pictured below c. 1914). A fire, believed to be caused by a damaged flue, started in the attic on March 9, 1914. (both JIM.)

The Solterra fire created such a commotion that the schoolhouse for employees' children released the students for the day. Attempts to extinguish the flames of the predominantly wood structure were futile. However, since the house burned from the attic downward, most of the furnishings were rescued. By the end of the day, the cottage, which 15 years earlier hosted the president of the United States, was nothing but charred fireplaces and smoldering ash. These pictures were taken c. 1914. (both JIM.)

Walter Furness (m. 1886–1901), employed by his uncle's architectural firm, Furness, Evans, & Company, also built a cottage in 1890. The architect designs of his uncle, Frank Furness, were very popular with wealthy industrialists, but considered radical and unconventional by some. The cottage was sold in 1896 to publisher Joseph Pulitzer (m. 1886–1911). Mr. Furness, an avid hunter, eventually resigned from the club due to an eye injury. The picture seen here is dated c. 1890s. (JIM.)

In 1897, after the completion of a larger home, Mr. Pulitzer used the Furness Cottage for employee housing, seen here c. 1890s. Around the end of 1913, John J. Albright obtained the cottage and used it for his employees as well. By 1929, Frank Goodyear Jr. (m. 1916–30), a lumber executive, purchased the home and donated it in honor of his mother for use as an infirmary. The small hospital was relocated away from the other cottages and staffed by a nurse, earning $150 a month in 1933. (JIM.)

Gordon Mckay (m. 1891–1903), an inventor, erected a cottage in 1892, seen here c. 1903. Mr. Mckay designed a sewing machine capable of stitching together all parts of a shoe. He amassed a fortune by cleverly leasing the machines to shoe manufacturers. His cousin, Wirt Dexter (m. 1886–90), a lawyer, was also a member. After the death of Mr. Mckay, William Rockefeller, a Standard Oil Company executive, acquired the house. Mr. Rockefeller, a younger brother of John D. Rockefeller, named the cottage Indian Mound because of a Native American refuge pile in the front yard. (JIM.)

During the Rockefeller occupancy, several construction alterations were made to the cottage. Changes included the addition of circular-shaped chambers, a larger porch encircling the home, a port-cochere (covered carriage entrance), and the shifting of fireplaces. In 1924, Helen Hartley Jenkins (m. 1909–34), a Remington Arms Manufacturing Company heir, bought the residence, seen here c. 1925. (JIM.)

William Rockefeller (seen right) with his wife, Almira, was instrumental in expanding the Standard Oil Company's international markets. Several Standard Oil partners' children were club members, including Edward Harkness (m. 1911–23), Robert Brewster, George Brewster (m. 1919–36), and Walter Jennings (m. 1926–33). Mr. Rockefeller's main membership influence was James Stillman (m. 1892–1918), president of National City Bank. National City Bank was the primary banking company used by Standard Oil. (Courtesy of the Rockefeller Archive Center.)

Helen Hartley Jenkins (seen left), *c.* 1925, inherited a large percentage of the Remington Arms and U.M.C. manufacturing company from her father, Marcellus Hartley. Mr. Hartley, although never a member, was on the finance committee of Henry Hyde's (m.1886–99) Equitable Life Assurance Company and formed the International Banking Corporation with Thomas Hubbard (m. 1904–15). In 1907, Mrs. Jenkins's nephew, Marcellus Hartley Dodge, married William Rockefellers's daughter Geraldine. (JIM.)

The above picture is dated c. 1896, and the below c. 1903. The Sans Souci apartment building was constructed in 1896. Translated from french as "without care," the structure had three floors with two apartments on each level and a fourth floor comprising 12 servant rooms. Occasionally leased to other members, an apartment could be rented for $25 a day in 1899. The first Sans Souci owners were William Anderson (m. 1888–97), retired president of the American Cotton Oil Company; Joseph Stickney (m. 1886–1903), a partner in the coal firm Stickney, Conyngham & Company; James Scrymser (m. 1894–1918), president of the Central and South America Telegraph Company; William Rockefeller; Henry Hyde; and J.P. Morgan. (both JIM.)

William Struthers (m. 1887–90, 1895–1911) and his wife, Savannah, built a cottage in 1896. Mr. Struthers was retired from William Struthers and Company, a firm manufacturing monuments, mantels, and interior decorations. Their cottage, named Moss, pictured here c. 1903, was occasionally used by Mr. Struthers's sister Helen and her husband, Rudolph Ellis (m. 1886–1915), a banker. The Struthers died within a month of each other in 1911, and their daughter Jean and her husband, Henry Sears (m. 1905–10), sold Moss cottage to George Macy (m. 1902–18). Mr. Macy was president of the Union Pacific Tea Company, a position eventually taken over by his son William (m. 1921–30, A.M.). George Macy, as well as his cousin, Valentine E. Macy (m. 1909-27), inherited wealth from Josiah Macy's Sons Merchant Company. (JIM.)

This picture is dated c. 1903. A cottage constructed in 1897 by Joseph Pulitzer was enlarged several times. It was once enlarged in 1899 by a multi-room addition, attached to the original home by a corridor, and again in 1904 with still more chambers, including a billiards room. Sensitive to sound, Mr. Pulitzer had his bedroom modified to include sound-deafening insulation and two doors on the entrance to reduce noise penetration. Further, the valet bedroom near his room used a muffled buzzer instead of a bell on the servants' call box. Mr. Pulitzer died in 1911, and his son Ralph (m. 1912–14) sold the cottage around 1913 to John J. Albright. (both JIM.)

Joseph Pulitzer (above left) successfully operated the *St. Louis Post-Dispatch*, as well as New York City's most widely read paper, the *World* . For all of the attention and expense lavished on the cottage, his wife, Kate (above right), disliked the island and seldom vacationed on Jekyll. (Courtesy of the Pulitzer family.)

A favorite island recreation for Mr. Albright and his second wife, Susan (both seen right), was bird watching. Their children enjoyed collecting sea shells and proudly displayed their finds in two glass-doored cabinets inside the cottage. Mr. Albright, originally a coal distributor, diversified into hydroelectric power and co-owned with Edmund Hayes half of the Westinghouse Company. Briefly, Mr. Albright and his brother-in-law, Amzi Barber (m. 1901–03), operated an asphalt paving business. (JIM.)

David H. King Jr. (m. 1889–1903), a building contractor, erected a cottage in 1897. Mr. King's contracting projects, among others, included the Statue of Liberty foundation and a large townhouse complex in Harlem. His cottage was purchased in 1901 by Edwin Gould (m. 1899–1933), who named it Chicota. This picture was taken c. 1910s. (JIM.)

Edwin Gould (seen left) and his brother George (m. 1895–1916) inherited a fortune from their father's railroad estate. Until the tragic death of Mr. Gould's son Edwin Jr. (m. 1914–17) in an island hunting accident, his family enjoyed sojourning on Jekyll regularly. After the incident, Mrs. Gould refused to visit and Mr. Gould vacationed infrequently. However, their other son Frank (m. 1924–45) had such fond memories of the island that he ultimately became a member and built a cottage near Chicota. (JIM.)

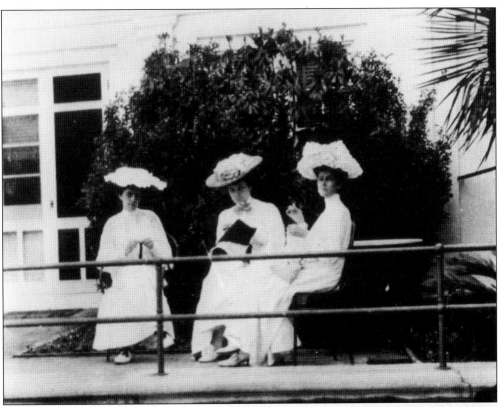

A unique feature of Chicota was a swimming pool located in the cottage atrium. Above, Sarah Gould, sitting far right with friends, engages in needlework by the swimming pool edge. Below, swimmers brave the pool's cold water, which was supplied by an artesian well. (both JIM.)

The Goulds constructed a dock in 1901, which became a prime place for crabbing and fishing. A boathouse was erected on the shore adjacent to it, and, at the end of the dock, a small storage house for canoes was built. (JIM.)

In the above c. 1914 picture, you can see that the front entrance of Chicota was framed by two stone lions. Unlike the other members' multi-storied cottages, this home was only one level. By the 1930s, Chicota was no longer used, and, in 1941, George Cowman Sr., a building contractor, dismantled the cottage. He used pieces of the structure to build a home for his family in Fancy Bluff, an area located near Brunswick. (JIM.)

In 1900, Henry K. Porter (m. 1891–1921), president of H.K. Porter Company, and his wife, Annie, constructed Mistletoe Cottage. This picture is dated c. 1903. H.K. Porter Company manufactured light steam locomotives. Mr. Porter was well known at the time as a leader in giving employee benefits, such as profit sharing and shorter work days. Also interested in politics, he served for one term as a Pennsylvania representative. John Claflin purchased the cottage in 1924. (JIM.)

John Claflin (far right), consorting with friends in this c. 1890 picture, was renowned for his traveling adventures. Mr. Claflin began his association with Jekyll before the formation of the club. In 1885, he and his wife, Elizabeth, enjoyed a day of hunting and picnicking on the island as the guest of John Eugene du Bignon. Mr. Claflin, his brother Authur (m. 1889–1904), and his cousin, Edward Eames (m. 1886–1901), were partners in the dry goods business, H.B. Claflin Company. (JIM.)

The cottage seen here *c*. 1904 was built for Edwin Gould's in-laws, Dr. George (m. 1904–07) and Hester Shrady (m. 1908–16). Dr. Shrady, besides operating a large private practice, was employed by numerous hospitals and was editor of two medical journals. He also witnessed the first prisoner electrocution and afterwards condemned the procedure. (JIM.)

In 1925, Dr. Walter Belknap James (m. 1917–27) and his wife, Helen (m. 1926–42), acquired the Shrady cottage and named it Cherokee, possibly after the Cherokee roses found on the island. Dr. James, a medical professor at Columbia University, inherited wealth from his father's lumber firm as did his brother Norman (m. 1918–31) and his sister, who married Allan McClane (m. 1924–28). The James's daughter Eunice married Henry Coe (m. 1925–34). This picture is dated *c*. 1929. (JIM.)

This picture can be dated to the early 1900s. A cottage was completed in 1906 for Frank Goodyear (m. 1902–07), president of the Great Southern Lumber Company and director in the New Orleans Great Northern Railroad. Mr. Goodyear ingeniously moved ahead of his lumber competitors by transporting timber to the sawmills by railway instead of seasonal waterways. Unfortunately, Mr. Goodyear died in 1907, but his wife, Josephine (m. 1909–15), became a member and took charge of the cottage. Upon her death, Frank Jr. inherited the house, and with his wife, Dorothy, enjoyed many happy seasons on the island. In 1932, two years after Frank Jr.'s death, Dorothy Goodyear and her new husband, Edmund P. Rogers (m. 1932–41), a banker, were vacationing in the cottage. (JIM.)

The club enclosure could be surveyed from the watertank tower. Scanning southward, in the early 1900s picture above, and northward, below, a view of the cottage layout is seen. (both JIM.)

On the site where Solterra cottage originally stood, Richard T. Crane Jr. (m. 1912–31) and his wife, Florence (m. 1919–40), erected a majestic Mediterranean-style home in 1917. Before construction, a member complained that the design was ostentatious and that its size would dominate the clubhouse. The member's opinion of the cottage, however, did not reflect the attitude toward the Cranes who were well liked by the majority of members. (JIM.)

Richard T. Crane Jr., seated far right, became president of the Crane Company after his older brother Charles (m. 1916–24) retired from the position to devote more time working as a diplomat. The Crane Company primarily manufactured plumbing items such as enameled fixtures, valves, and fittings. After the death of Mr. Crane, his wife, Florence, seated second from right, became owner of the cottage. (JIM.)

A reflecting pool highlighted the main entrance landscaping, and, by the mid-1920s, climbing fig plants created a foliage facade on the walls of Crane cottage. Motorized transportation on the island included cars and "Red Bugs," both seen parked in front of the cottage. (JIM.)

Curtained loggias and arched entranceways framed the Crane cottage courtyard. A fountain was located in the center. (JIM.)

The Crane Cottage was decorated with Italian-style antiques. The lighting fixtures in the living room, seen above, *c.* 1920s, were wrought-iron reproductions reputedly manufactured in Italy. One of the bedrooms, seen below, contained a small canopied bed with Italian ladder-back chairs. (both JIM.)

Walter (m. 1926–33) and Jean Jennings (m. 1934–41) built a cottage in 1927. They named the home Villa Ospo, a name reflecting early 20th-century history. Some anthropologists in the 1920s believed Jekyll Island was the area described in 16th-century Spanish documents as Ospo, a coastal Native American community. (JIM.)

Walter Jennings, a director in Standard Oil, had numerous family relations in the club. For example, his sisters Helen James, Emma Auchincloss (m. 1932–42), and Annie Jennings (m. 1938–39) were all members. Further, their father was related to the Goulds, and their maternal aunt and uncle were William and Almira Rockefeller. (JIM.)

Villa Ospo's tiled corridor, seen above, c. 1928, led from the living room to the main entrance. The entryway was adorned by a 17th-century Spanish door, and an antique Spanish lantern complemented the foyer. In addition, antique doors decorated with richly painted still lifes were used throughout the cottage. (JIM.)

The living room decor of family photographs, Arab-influenced Spanish ceramics, and other personal items created an atmosphere of comfort in this c. 1928 picture. Cut flowers and potted plants were also arranged throughout the room. The desk, far right, was used by Mrs. Jennings, and the desk to the left, behind the sofa, was used by Mr. Jennings. (JIM.)

In 1928, Frank M. Gould (m. 1924–45) and his first wife, Florence, erected a cottage. The picture seen here is dated *c.* 1930. Named after their daughter Marianne, Villa Marianna was the last home built by a member. By the 1920s along Plantation Road, Cherokee roses were trained up the trunks of the cabbage palmettos and across lines attached between the trees. (JIM.)

Frank Gould, who inherited wealth from his father, Edwin, had the cottage grounds landscaped with courtyards and fountains. At the death of Frank Gould, his second wife's lawyer, Lawrence Condon (m. 1946–47), obtained the Gould's island assets and reputedly lived in Villa Marianna at the time the state of Georgia purchased Jekyll. This picture was taken *c.* 1930s. (JIM.)

Two
CLUB ACTIVITIES

"The world of industry and commerce, of railroads and factories, of trusts, mergers, and monopolies, is something wholly apart from this island paradise."—Munsey Magazine, February 1904. (Courtesy of the Coastal Georgia Historical Society.)

By the 1890s, church services were offered weekly by either regional clergy or prominent ministers, including, at times, sermons by Reverend Charles H. Parkhurst (m. 1894–1909), the only honorary club member. The Union Chapel (seen left), c. 1899, was built around 1897, however, it was soon realized that the interdenominational church was too small for the needs of the club. It was relocated in 1903 to the Quarters, a group of houses used by employees of African descent, and served as the church for the club's black workers. (JIM)

In 1904, Faith Chapel (seen right) c. 1940s, was erected where the Union Chapel originally stood. Quite different from the first church, Faith Chapel included ornamental features, such as belfry gargoyles and stained-glass windows, one of which was installed by Louis Comfort Tiffany. Besides worship services, the church was used for baptisms, funerals, several employee weddings, and one wedding for a member's family. Charles and Charlotte Maurice's daughter Emily married Charles Dall at Faith Chapel on December 19, 1911. (JIM.)

Festooned with garlands, a table in this early 1900s picture was exquisitely prepared for a multi-course banquet, and, as expected for a dinner, the members and guests wore formal attire. Although not of the clubhouse dining room, this photograph is a wonderful example of an evening meal. (JIM.)

After dinner, members could choose from card playing, billiards, or, as seen to the right, c. 1941, conversations in one of the clubhouse parlors. Occasionally, impromptu, as well as planned dances took place, and, in 1900, a debate occurred over whether or not to add a dancing floor in the smoking parlor. (Courtesy of the *Saturday Evening Post*.)

Smoking a pipe in this *c.* 1928 picture, Jack Franklin, a guest, peruses a newspaper on the clubhouse veranda. Besides pipes, many members enjoyed smoking cigars but only if they were light ones. In 1898, over 300 dark cigars were returned by the club to the distributor in exchange for a lighter type. (Courtesy of the Coastal Georgia Historical Society.)

Teas, an everyday habit for some of the members, were prepared and served by dining room waiters. In the *c.* 1926 picture above, from left to right, Charles S. Brown (m. 1924–35); William F. Morgan's (m. 1925–34, A.M.) wife, Emma; Mrs. Bill Armour; and Frederick Snow (m. 1915–18, 1925–29) have tea on the clubhouse veranda. Ninety teas were served at the clubhouse during March of 1926. (Courtesy of the Coastal Georgia Historical Society.)

Above, c. 1901, a picnic took place on the beach to celebrate the opening of the season. Wooden tables were erected and participants lounged, some elegantly with parasols, near the sand dunes. (JIM.)

An enjoyable activity, weather permitting, was partaking in a picnic. With a Poland water bottle and basket in hand, Dr. I. Ridgeway Trimble and Mary Beard pose on the clubhouse veranda, c. 1931. Dr. Trimble was employed as the club physician during the 1931 season. Mary Beard was the daughter of Anson Beard (m. 1927–29) and the granddaughter of James J. (m. 1888–1916) and Mary Hill (m. 1916–21). Mr. Hill was president of the Great Northern Railroad Co. (Courtesy of the Coastal Georgia Historical Society.)

Above, c. 1921, a picnic took place near the area where Shell Road terminated at the beach. Shell Road was the main access from the club enclosure to the ocean. Below, the same picnic, which included William Rockefeller and Dr. Walter James, is seen from a closer view. The bathing cabin, seen in the background, was a building divided into several swimwear changing rooms. (both JIM.)

The Cranes hosted a barbecue, seen above in this c. 1929 picture, in the woods north of the club enclosure. Members often participated in cookouts in the forest, as well as along the beach. On one occasion, entertainment for an oyster roast was provided by African-American fiddle players. During the same event, members young and old danced the Virginia Reel. (JIM.)

Some social gatherings took place around the cottages. Above, the Porter's soiree at their home, Mistletoe, was complete with ground cover, chairs, and umbrellas, c. early 1900s. (JIM.)

Sporting contests, called, by some participants, gymkhanas, were held almost yearly on the beach. Winners received a prize. Competitions included foot, three-legged, sack, egg, bicycle, and "Red Bug" races. Supposedly horse racing was attempted one year, however, it was too chaotic and was canceled thereafter. Club members' children, above, in the early 1900s, prepare for a race involving the use of spoons. (JIM.)

John J. Albright's children, from left to right, Nancy, Susan, Fuller, and Betty play in the sand, c. 1910s. Although normally too cold to swim in the ocean during January or February, opportunities often existed by March. (JIM.)

John J. Albright's granddaughter, Nancy Hurd (left), and Frank Gould's daughter Marianne, rest on the beach, c. 1930. (JIM.)

In 1898, during the Spanish-American War, the United States erected gun batteries on the northern and southern extremities of Jekyll. Parrott cannons, dating from the 1860s, were eventually placed on the south end battery. Although the war only lasted about three months, the guns were not removed until April of 1900. Above, members and guest investigate one of the cannons, c. 1899. (JIM.)

In the early years, a horse and carriage was a necessity for traversing the island pathways, and, although many of the members brought their own coaches to Jekyll, rigs, complete with a liveried driver, were available on a rental basis from the club stables. Seen left, c. 1903, a horse and carriage takes advantage of the north end beach at low tide. (JIM.)

A liveried driver c. 1914, takes the Albright's children, Nancy and Susan, and their nurse, Carey Riley, on a carriage ride through the ocean waves. During night excursions, the sisters often enjoyed searching for wild hogs and deer with a flashlight. (JIM.)

Some members preferred using saddled horses over carriages. In the early 1900s picture above, Susan Albright rides a horse while her sister Nancy sits on a bicycle. Master Keyes (far right) was employed as the Albright's coachman. (JIM)

Horse and carriages were also used during hunting expeditions. Above, Duncan Steuart Ellsworth's wife, Jane, steps down from a buckboard carriage with a shotgun resting on her shoulder, c. 1899. (JIM.)

In the c. 1899 picture above, Jane Ellsworth and a hunting guide view a retrieved bird. Mrs. Ellsworth, during her visit in 1899, shot over 27 quail and a pheasant. Originally, the club's principal attraction was hunting, and they were adamant that all shooters register any game killed in a book. (JIM)

Upland rice and other grains were planted around several island ponds in hope of luring ducks and other birds to the region. In later years, hunters hid behind shooting blinds and set out duck decoys. For the anglers, bait and tackle were available from the club office, and fishing platforms were located on the north end creek. While vacationing in 1917, it was recorded that George Macy caught over 20 bass. This picture is dated c. 1930s. (JIM.)

Two unidentified men, *c.* 1920, the one standing right possibly Charles Maurice's son George, display a shot deer. Members desiring to hunt had to follow the club's hunting rules, and any infraction resulted in a $5 fine. Rules included a ban on loaded weapons being carried within the clubhouse grounds, and animals, such as singing and plumage birds, could not be killed. (JIM.)

This alligator, *c.* 1903, was captured and temporarily kept near the club enclosure. Besides alligators and deer, other animals hunted included quail, pheasants, turkeys, ducks, wild hogs, rabbits, and raccoons. (JIM.)

This picture is dated *c.* 1899. Shooting events periodically took place, and on at least one occasion, platforms (seen left) were erected for competition. After several seasons, it was realized that the island was being over-hunted. To combat this problem, thousands of dollars were spent stocking the island. Mongolian pheasants, raised by the gamekeeper, were released along with imported quail, deer, and turkeys. (JIM.)

James Scrymser leans over the shoulder of an unidentified man, possibly John J. Albright, during a shooting competition, *c.* 1899. By the 1910s, restrictive game laws made it difficult to purchase animals for stocking the island, and the Mongolian pheasants were not enough to satisfy the hunting taking place. The gamebook illustrates the situation. During the 1900 season, 2774 quail and 54 pheasants were killed while hunting, but by the 1910 season, only 601 quail and 9 pheasants were shot. (JIM.)

Hunting became so lousy that, in 1916, Dr. Frederick Shattuck (m. 1912–29) jokingly inscribed in the gamebook that the only thing he killed was a mosquito. In later years, hunting was limited to either duckshooting on Latham Hammock, a small island owned by Frank Gould and located between Jekyll and the mainland, or traveling to cabin bluff, a preserve managed by the Sea Island Company. The picture seen here is *c.* 1899. (JIM.)

This sketshooting field was built in 1936. The field opened daily at 3 p.m., and, on Saturdays, competitions were staged for the members. A round of shooting with a .410 gauge shotgun in 1941 cost $2.60. (JIM.)

Possibly at the end of Shell Road, in the c. 1899 picture above, members and spouses rest from bicycling. By the 1890s, bicycles were the island rave, and their popularity remained strong up to the final club season. (JIM.)

Through funding provided by various members, several pathways of crushed oyster shells were built for the exclusive use of bicycles. In 1898, William Rockefeller paid for the construction of a bike path, seen above, c. 1903, that stretched south from Shell Road, parallel to the beach. (JIM.)

A bike in 1941 could be rented from the club for either $5 a week, $1 a day, or 50¢ an hour. If a member brought their own, the club offered care and storage for $1.50 a week. In the early 1900s picture above, from left to right, the Albright children, John Jr., Fuller, and Elizabeth, ride bicycles behind the clubhouse annex. (JIM.)

From left to right, c. 1928, Mrs. Allan McLane and Mrs. Jean Jennings take a leisurely ride on velocipedes within the club enclosure. Adult tricycles were privately owned by some of the cottage families. (Courtesy of the Coastal Georgia Historical Society.)

In the late 1910s a small open-aired vehicle named the Red Bug was introduced to the Jekyll Island Club. Chris Nielsen, the club's carpenter in the 1910s and early 1920s, discovered Red Bugs while searching for a company manufacturing small-sized wheels. Nielsen, constructing a bicycle for his son David, obtained wheels from Briggs and Stratton. This business used the wheels on a small-motorized transport called the Flyer, the Red Bug's first name. Above, Red Bugs are viewed during the 1925 season on the beach near Shell Road. (Courtesy of the Coastal Georgia Historical Society.)

A fifth wheel, powered by an engine, was located at the rear of the gasoline Red Bug and allowed the vehicle to reach speeds of up to 25 mph. Originally designed for use as an economical car, the gasoline version was replaced by 1925 with the slower operating electric model. At left c. 1929, club member Helen H. Jenkins and Dr. Ronald MacEarchern of Johns Hopkins Hospital are seen standing beside an electric Red Bug. (JIM.)

Lawrence Hurd, the son-in-law of club member John J. Albright, is pictured at right riding a Red Bug on the beach during the 1930 season. Although it was often used as an amusement park ride, electric Red Bugs could be purchased throughout the United States as well as in Europe. In France it was marketed as Le Red Bug. In America, a 1928 Red Bug advertisement in *Country Life* magazine explained, "It operates on standard automobile storage batteries, rechargeable in your own garage or at any service station. It is fully equipped with emergency brake and parking lock. Red Bug has powerful headlights and taillight for night driving, and [a] standard automobile horn." (JIM.)

A row of Red Bugs, possibly parked behind the club's garage and stable building, are viewed above in the 1920s or 1930s. Although the club possessed numerous electric and gasoline Red Bugs for the use of members and guests, many of the families opted to buy their own. In 1941 the club offered Red Bugs for rent at $3 a day or $20 for the week. Privately owned Red Bugs could be stored in the garage and maintained for 50¢ a day. For comparison, the club rented a chauffered automobile for $5 an hour. (JIM.)

The club's first golf course, constructed in 1898, was located north of the clubhouse between the enclosure fence and Wylly Road. Being of a simplistic nature, it was replaced in 1909 by a larger course positioned on the oceanside of the island. A golfer (seen above), c. 1910s, putts on the 10th hole of the second course. (JIM.)

Walter Travis, a golf professional, was engaged in 1926 to redesign the oceanside golf course. By 1928, an 18-hole course, compared to links found in Scotland, was ready for play. Lessons were available from golf experts employed by the club, and caddies could be hired to carry golf bags. (JIM.)

The above picture is dated *c.* 1930s, and the below is *c.* early 1930s. A tea house, overlooking the ocean, was located on the golf course. Refreshments were available for golfers as well as non-golfers, and if desired, clubhouse waiters served tea at the structure. During March of 1929, 101 teas were given at the building. Furnished with a film projector and sound equipment, the club presented movies at the Tea House on a regular basis. (above–JIM, below–Courtesy of Roberta From.)

An unidentified woman swings a club in front of the Tea House (above) and the golf shed. The Tea House, probably built in the early 1910s, was moved in the 1920s to the sand dunes near the ocean. The golf shed, located on the golf course near Shell Road, was used to store golfing supplies and members' golf clubs. (JIM.)

Richard T. Crane Jr. practices his golf putt on the grounds near his cottage. A putting green was located near the clubhouse, and in the late 1930s, putting contests were held weekly. (JIM.)

By the 1910s, golf tournaments were held annually. This picture is dated *c.* 1938. Members competed for trophies, including the Presidents Cup, donated in 1916 by Frederick Bourne, and the Morgan Cup, given in the 1930s by J.P. Morgan Jr. On one occasion, an exhibition game with professional golfer Sam Snead took place. (JIM.)

By the 1930s, contests such as "monkey golf," seen above, *c.* 1941, were played. "Monkey golf" was a game in which groups of eight to ten players, each using only one club, competed for the lowest score against other teams. Standing third from right, with his left hand touching his head, is possibly Robert Gardner (A.M.), an investment broker with Mitchell-Hutchins & Company. (Courtesy of the *Saturday Evening Post*.)

Another highly popular sport on Jekyll was the game of tennis. Scheduling a playing time on the clubhouse lobby's registration sheet was strongly encouraged. Seen left, c. 1929, Helen H. Jenkins's personal secretary, Charles Fremd, poses on one of the tennis courts. (JIM.)

With avid tennis players such as Julian Myrick (A.M.), former president of the U.S. Lawn Tennis Association, and Bernon Prentice, former chair of the Davis Cup Commission, the club made sure its courts were in great playing condition. Surfaced with native clay, two outdoor tennis courts were directly south of the clubhouse. By the late 1930s, a third court was added somewhere within the enclosure. This picture was taken c. 1937. (JIM.)

Stretching at the tennis courts are Richard T. Crane Jr.'s daughter Florence (standing right) and his niece, Florence Higgenbothem, c. 1929. Tennis lessons were available from a professional, who, from 1936–42, was Frank Bonneau. (JIM.)

A mixed doubles tennis tournament was held annually in which participants competed for the Crane Cup, a trophy donated in the early 1910s by R.T. Crane Jr. In later years, players in a junior mixed doubles tournament, the finals of which are seen above, also contended for a Crane Cup. Another tournament, a men's doubles round robin, was started in 1936. Competitors vied for a trophy given by Alanson Houghton (m. 1919–41), retired president of Corning Glass Ware and a former U.S. Ambassador. This picture is dated c. 1941. (JIM.)

Erected in 1929, an indoor tennis court, seen above, c. 1929, offered members and guests the opportunity of playing tennis during evenings and inclement weather. If using the structure at night, a charge was issued to pay for the electricity. In 1941, the fee was $5 an hour. Below, c. 1941, the mixed doubles Crane Cup tournament takes place inside the indoor court. (both JIM.)

Edwin Gould constructed a recreational building, seen in the *c.* 1903 photograph above, in 1902. Called the Gould Playhouse, the interior consisted of three bedrooms, two baths, a large living room, a shooting range, and two bowling alleys. In 1913, an indoor tennis court, with separate male and female dressing rooms, was added to the structure. Later improvements to the playhouse included a green house. (JIM.)

The Gould Playhouse bowling alleys (seen above), *c.* 1903, were manufactured by Brunswick-Balke-Collender. For many years, members had access to the building, particularly the tennis court; however, after 1920, the club could only use the court during tournaments. (JIM.)

By the 1920s, lawn bowling competitions were held weekly and a tournament occurred annually for the C.S. Brown Cup, a trophy donated by Charles S. Brown (m. 1924–35). Seen above, *c.* 1929, William F. Morgan, Charles M. Daniels (m.1924–32), William W. Vaughn, and either Bayard C. Hoppin (m.1925–31) or Gerard B. Hoppin (m.1923–38) bowl on the clubhouse lawns near the swimming pool. Below, *c.* 1940, in the same location as above, members and guests compete for the C.S. Brown Memorial Cup. (above–Courtesy of Coastal Georgia Historical Society, below–JIM.)

In July of 1925 a swimming pool was dug and poured near the main entranceway of the clubhouse. The swimming pool, seen above in the 1930s, replaced a small reflecting pool that had adorned the lawns since the early 1900s. For fun in the 1930s and early 1940s children of club members and guests often staged swim competitions. Below, teenagers and young adults sunbathe near the pool during the 1941 season. By March, the club typically placed smudge pots, a container with a smoldering and smoky fire, around the pool walkway to help deter insects. (above—JIM; below—Courtesy of the *Saturday Evening Post*.)

Adorned in outfits to keep away mosquitoes, Cornelius "Connie" Lee (m. 1919–47) and Michael Gavin (m. 1924–33), seen above, c. 1927, clown around near the swimming pool. Below, the joking soon results in both members becoming soaked. Connie Lee, a good friend of George Baker, was a self-employed New York stockbroker. Michael Gavin was married to Gertrude Hill, the daughter of railroad entrepreneur James J. Hill. (both–Courtesy of the Coastal Georgia Historical Society.)

The swimming pool was filled by an artesian well, and a diving board was located next to the diving tower. Seen right, c. 1941, Isabel, the daughter of A.J. Drexel Paul (m. 1927–33, A.M.), a banker, stands on the diving tower steps. Ms. Paul's great uncle was Lynford Biddle (m. 1928–33, A.M.). (Courtesy of the *Saturday Evening Post*.)

Wearing a coat and tie, David Ingalls (A.M.), a lawyer, stands near his wife, Louise Harkness, c. 1939, as she socializes with other swimmers. Mrs. Ingalls's father was a cousin to Edward Harkness. (JIM.)

Francis Jr., a son of Francis D. Bartow, rides a four-wheeled sailing vehicle on the beach, c.1938. The club owned a land sailer as early as the 1920s; however, sand and salt often caused the wheel bearings to lock up. (JIM.)

Flying to the island, c. early 1940s, David Ingalls landed a plane on the beach during low tide. Mr. Ingalls, a Navy pilot during WWI, was honored with the Distinguished Flying Cross and decorated by France with the U.S. Legion of Honor. (JIM.)

Three

CLUB EMPLOYEES AND SUPPORT STRUCTURES

"It was only three months out of the year that [the members were] there, the rest of the year, why only the employees had the use of the island. That's where I got my jump in golf, because the millionaires would use the golf course three months out of the year, the other nine months I would use it." — Earl Hill; Jekyll Island Club employee, c.1920s. (JIM.)

The club staffed the island with both seasonal and year-round employees. Seasonal employees, such as chambermaids and waiters, were hired primarily from resorts in the northeast, and they came to Brunswick by Mallory steamer from New York. Travel expenses were paid by the club. In 1898, a second-class ticket on a boat operated by the Mallory & Company steam line cost $15. Eventually, the railroad replaced the ship as the principle transportation for workers. From Brunswick, employees arrived to the island by using one of the club boats, seen above, and supplies, including horses and baggage, were pulled over, seen below, c. 1910s, by a scow. (both JIM.)

Workers often participated in dances, oyster roasts, and parties, but, due to segregation laws in effect during the club era, employees of African descent held their recreational activities separately. Above, *c.* 1909, club employees, as well as members' servants, participate in a St. Patrick's Day dance in Frederic Baker's stable. (JIM.)

During non-working hours, employees were able to use some of the island amenities, such as the beach and bicycle paths. Above, *c.* 1916, Thomas Gage, a contractor hired to build the Crane cottage, enjoys a day at the beach with his family. (JIM.)

Throughout the club's existence there was a constant influx of new employees. While some of the club's staff, such as the superintendent and steamship captain, retained their jobs for years, other employees, like the bellmen and waiters, worked from only one to a few seasons. In the above photograph, c. 1903, employees hired for the 1903 season spend time off from work on the beach. (JIM.)

Ernest Gilbert Grob, the club superintendent, playfully wrestles with Dr. Warfield Firor (standing left). Dr. Firor, from Johns Hopkins Hospital, earned $100 a month as the club's physician. Although employees, doctors were treated more like members. Ernest Grob was respected by both members and workers. Ever thoughtful, he often gave flowers to the women vacationing. For instance, at the end of President McKinley's visit in 1899, Mr. Grob had a basket of pink and white roses presented to the President's and Vice President's wives. (JIM.)

A son of Swiss immigrants, Ernest Grob (right), c. 1890, earned $3000 a year in 1904 as the superintendent. Mr. Grob's employment began in 1888 as a clerk in the clubhouse office. The following season, he was promoted to clubhouse manager, and, by 1890, he became the superintendent, retaining this position until his retirement in 1930. Superintendents before Mr. Grob were Richard Ogden (m. 1886–92) and H.M. Schley. (JIM.)

Mr. Grob stayed during the autumn at the club cottage (seen above), c. 1903, and prepared for the upcoming season. By January, he resided in the clubhouse. In the summer, Mr. Grob managed another resort in Maine, at first the Grindstone Inn, but later he switched to the Malvern Hotel. Many of the club's seasonal employees in the 1910s and 1920s also worked at the Malvern. Although he never married, two employees named a child after him, and his nephew, Newton Grobe (Grob's brother added an 'e' to the name to help others pronounce it correctly), worked at the club as a stenographer for two seasons and a bookkeeper for one. (JIM.)

Enjoying a beer with other employees, Michel L. De Zutter (sitting far right) was the club superintendent from 1930 to 1942. Mr. De Zutter, a Belgium immigrant, managed during the summer both The Blind Brook Club, a golfing and dining facility, and the Glen Island Casino, a music hall and dining room hosting famous performers, such as Glenn Miller and Benny Goodman. During the 1930s, many of the club's seasonal employees also worked at one of these places. By the mid-1930s, Eugene Flohr (sitting third from right) was employed as the chief electrical engineer. Rufus Bennett (standing third from right) was employed in 1939 in the boat department, but from the summer of 1942 to 1946 he was the island caretaker. Authur Le Blanc, a plumber, stands second from right. (Courtesy of Lillian Schaitberger.)

For years, John Etter, seen sitting with his son Howard was the club's assistant superintendent. In 1925, he earned $225 a month. Mr. Etter, the nephew of Ernest Grob's brother, also worked in the same capacity under Mr. Grob at the Malvern Hotel. Other assistant superintendents for the club included William Turner, Julius A. Falk, and Ernest Banwell. Mr. Etter's wife, Ray, seen with her son, John Marshall, was employed briefly as a chambermaid in the clubhouse. (JIM.)

By the 1910s, the office staff for the club consisted of a superintendent, an assistant superintendent, a bookkeeper, a day clerk, a night clerk, as well as a day telephone operator, an evening telephone operator, and a stenographer. Ernest Grob (standing left) c.1920, poses with Otto and Elizebeth Lederer during their wedding. During the late 1920s, Mr. Lederer earned $100 a month as an office clerk. Mrs. Lederer, before marrying, was a chambermaid for the Maurice family. (JIM.)

James A. Clark (on the motorcycle), c. 1926, was hired in 1888 to be the main steamship captain. In 1925, he earned $200 a month in this position. During at least one summer, Captain Clark was in charge of buying turtles caught by other year-round employees and storing them in the terrapin pen. The turtles were fed shrimp until the club season, at which time they became part of the dining room cuisine. (JIM.)

Around 1900, Captain Clark married Minnie Schuppan, the club's head housekeeper, and, in 1901, the home (seen above), c. 1903, was built for their use. After retiring in 1930, Mr. Clark continued to work briefly as the road inspector, reporting to Sim Denegal, the road foreman, any road repair work needed. Steamship captains hired in the 1930s included A. Alden and Joe Spaulding. (JIM.)

A typical season required the hiring of two boat captains, a boat engineer, two deckhands, a dockman, and a fireman. Richard Backus (seen above), c. 1932, was hired in 1931 to operate the club launch *Sylvia*. Launch captains employed during the 1920s and 1930s earned $90 a month. (JIM.)

During the 1920s the club employed two boat engineers, John Courier, and an assistant, James Harper (seen right), c.1928 or 1929. By 1930, Mr. Harper was the only boat engineer, earning a salary of $150 a month. During the 1930 season, his son, James Harper Jr., worked as a nightwatchman. (JIM.)

Above, c. 1910, from left to right, Louise Gross, Stella Thompson , and Ms. Carpenter stand in front of a palmetto tree. For many years, Ms. Gross worked as the head housekeeper at both the Jekyll Island Club and the Malvern Hotel. In 1925, the head housekeeper was paid $100 a month to manage the linenwoman, chambermaids, and cleaners. Others employed in this position included Kate Graf, Minnie Schuppan Clark, E.G. Hatzel, F. King, and Agnes Murray. Stella Thompson was the daughter of the south end fisherman and guard, J. Henry Thompson. (JIM.)

Above, c. 1918, club employees and spouses stand in front of the mule shed for a wedding photograph. Ray Marshall Etter (third from right) and Roseta Marshall Flanders (second from right), along with Marianne Marshall Cameron, were sisters employed in the 1910s as chambermaids on Jekyll as well as at the Malvern Hotel. Like many of the staff members, the sisters married co-workers they met while employed on the island. (JIM.)

Every season, seven to ten chambermaids were engaged to take care of responsibilities such as making the beds and placing clean towels in the clubhouse rooms. In 1925, a chambermaid's salary was $30 a month. At right, *c.* early 1920s, Marie Clark, a chambermaid, sits at the top of the children's playhouse slide with two unidentified employees. The playhouse was located near Shell Road and the beach. (JIM)

The club hired about ten cleaners a season to dust, sweep, and mop the rooms of the clubhouse. In 1936, Carrie Maxwell (left), *c.* 1930s, earned $20 a month working in this position. Ms. Maxwell's father, Shepard Maxwell, was a forest laborer for the club, and her mother, Bell, was the sister of Charlie and Myers Hill, both of whom were longtime club employees. (JIM.)

By the 1920s, a messenger, two porters, and six bellmen were under the club's employ. Albert Murphy (left), c. 1920s, poses in a bellman uniform. Bellmen, working in shifts, waited in the office until their services were needed. In 1925, a bellman earned $35 a month. While bellmen carried light luggage, delivered items, and raised and lowered the clubhouse tower flag, it was the porter's duty to transport heavy trunks. (JIM.)

Above, c. early 1900s, George Harvey, standing far right with a group of waiters, was one of two waiters involved in a drowning on Jekyll on March 21, 1912. Mr. Harvey and Hector Deliyannis, the other waiter involved in the incident, were buried on the island. The local burial was probably due to both being immigrants and their nearest relatives residing overseas. (JIM.)

For the 1925 season, the club hired a headwaiter, 17 waiters, and three busmen to work in the dining room. A cafe clerk, the name given by the club for the bartender, was employed as well. Above, c. 1937, waiters in uniform gather near the Crane cottage for a group photograph. Carl Puls (standing center in a dark suit) was the headwaiter, earning $175 a month in 1938. (JIM.)

In 1899, meals could be sent to clubhouse rooms or to cottages for an extra 50¢ above the regular price. However, supposedly by the 1930s only breakfast was offered for delivery to the cottages. Above, c. 1937, Eric Wylie (standing right) and two other waiters transport food using a tricycle equipped with a metal container for holding trays. Mr. Wylie, earning $80 a month in 1937, also worked for the Glen Island Casino. (JIM.)

In 1889, a dormitory, seen above, *c.* 1910s, was constructed for the use of single white employees such as bellmen, chefs, and waiters. The building, called the White Servants Annex, consisted of three levels. Most of the workers resided two to a room. Black employees, such as laundry attendants, kitchen helpers, and personal staff of club members, lived in what was called the Colored Servants Annex, a two-storied dormitory adjacent to the White Servants Annex. In 1925, the annex for blacks caught fire and burned down. It was replaced by renovating the Gould Stable and turning it into a dormitory. (JIM.)

Above, *c.* 1910s, unidentified employees eat watermelon by the White Servants Annex porch. The first floor of the dormitory had a large room used for employee parties. By the 1920s, movies were presented in the same area. Movies were shown to both blacks and whites; however, due to segregation, the groups watched films on different nights. In an attempt to deter younger men from gambling at the sleeping quarters, J.P. Morgan Jr., in 1927, purchased a radio for the workers, and the club constructed a library for the employees' use. The bench on the porch is possibly a pew from the church. (JIM.)

Employees, probably waiters, dress in palmetto fronds and pose by a shed on the beach, c. early 1930s. The shed was possibly used to store beach chairs. (Courtesy of Roberta From.)

This picture is dated c. 1930s. The club was adamant about the dining room fare being of the highest quality, and, to insure this standard, the best chefs available were hired. In 1925, the chef earned $210 a month and the pastry chef $175 a month. Their entourage included a second cook, roast cook, fry cook, butcher, bread baker, pastry helper, and a vegetable preparer. Also included on the kitchen staff were a pot washer, silverman, five dishwashers, a glass washer, fireman, steward, and three storeroom attendants. (Courtesy of Roberta From.)

By 1930, a Married Servants Annex, seen above, was erected near the White Servants Annex. The structure, seen left of the annex, was a library used by the workers. Below, c. early 1930s, employees gather in the Married Servants Annex living room. Pianos were a popular form of entertainment for employees as well as members. (both Courtesy of Roberta From.)

Waitresses were hired to work in several different areas. Some served meals to seasonal workers in the employee's dining room, located in the clubhouse basement, and others waited on member's children and their caretakers in the nurses hall, located on the clubhouse first floor. Above, c. early 1930s, Christine Morney Thuris was a waitress employed to operate the Tea House. Her husband, Robert, the headwaiter during 1931 and 1932, manufactured gin, vodka, and bourbon for the club during Prohibition. Their bourbon was actually alcohol, reputedly smuggled in from Canada, colored with prune juice. (Courtesy of Roberta From.)

In 1938, Dorethea Mitchell (above) earned $25 a month as a waitress in the Mess Hall. The Mess Hall, constructed by the 1930s, was used as a dining facility for employees living in the boarding house. Ms. Mitchell's father, Leonard, was a forest laborer for the club and her mother, Evelyn, was a cleaner in the housekeeping department. (JIM.)

In 1925, Samuel "Sim" Denegal (seen left) earned $100 a month as the forest foreman. Mr. Denegal was in charge of 15 to 18 men hired to clear debris, repair bridges, and spread oyster shells on roads. The shells were crushed by using a heavy mule-pulled roller. Mr. Denegal's second wife, Elizabeth, occasionally worked as a cook, and two of his sons, Scott and Walter, were employed as laborers. (JIM.)

Some of the black employees with families lived in an area of the enclosure called the Quarters, five houses constructed in a semi-circle pattern. Sim Denegal lived there and operated an off-season commissary near his home. By the 1930s, the commissary, selling everything from flour to cigarettes, operated in the winter as well. At right, two young men playfully jab each other in front of the entrance to Denegal's commissary. (JIM.)

Famous for his bellowing laughter, John Cain (above), c. 1914, was hired to perform duties such as deliver coal and wood to the cottages and cart oyster shells to roads and bicycle paths. Married to Sarah Hill, his brothers-in-law, Charlie and Myers Hill, were two longtime employees. Tragically, Mr. Cain died in the early 1920s. Supposedly, while alongside a wagon, lightning spooked the club's mules, Pete and Julia, and jammed him between a tree and the wheel of the hitched wagon. (JIM.)

Located on the island's north end were the ruins of a home built during English colonization for Maj. William Horton, seen here c. 1903. Dubbed by the club as "Old Tabby," the walls of the structure were restored in 1898 by 23 of the members who contributed $27 each to the preservation cause. (JIM.)

Ten to 12 groundskeepers were hired to maintain the enclosure lawns, as well as assist porters in moving heavy items. The foremen in the early years were of European descent, but, by the 1920s, men of African descent held the position. The 1920s also saw the addition of a flower gardener who, for many years, was Wesley Wellman. Groundskeepers and forest employees without families on the island lived in the Camp, a bunkhouse built near the Quarters. This picture is dated *c*.1903. (JIM.)

A garden, staffed by a gardener and two assistants, was cultivated seasonally to help supply the dining room with vegetables such as brusselsprouts, carrots, and peas. Above, *c*. early 1900s, the vegetable garden is seen from the water tower. The home in the distance was used by the family of Torkel "Chips" Torkelson, a carpenter for the club in the early years. A second garden, located behind the mule shed and garage, was used to grow feed for the livestock. (JIM.)

JEKYLL ISLAND CAMPGROUND
1197 RIVERVIEW DRIVE
JEKYLL ISLAND
GA 31527
0
Phone: 1-912-635-3021
Fax:

Qty	Item	Price	Extended
1	JEKYLL ISLAND S		
		18.99	18.99
	Disc.		-3.80

	Subtotal	18.99
	Discount	-3.80
Tax		0.91

| | Total | 16.10 |
| | Amt Received | 16.10 |

| | Chg Due | 0.00 |
| Paid with: | | CASH |

Signature.................

Reg #:   S00103010931
CR#: S00103040690
Printed: DEC 21 03-9:51 AM
Clerk: ALICE MONROE

Thank You

The club typically hired a greenskeeper, an assistant, and eight to ten men to maintain the golf course. Scott Denegal, pictured right, was employed on the greenskeeping staff to perform tasks such as mowing the greens and raking the sand traps. In 1938, he earned $2 a day. In the early years, the greenskeepers were of European descent, but, by the 1930s, they were of African descent. (JIM.)

Consulting Sim Denegal, the club realized it needed more housing for forest, ground, and golf laborers, who were residing at the Camp but caring for families off the island. To solve this problem, ten houses, seen above, were constructed in 1916 near the Quarters. Called Red Row, the roof and exterior walls of the dwelling were covered with red-rolled roofing. (JIM.)

Every season, coal was delivered to the dock, and the employees working in the grounds and forest crews unloaded the vessel. Because of the quantity ordered, 1000 tons in 1916, coal removal and storage took at least a week to complete. Standing right, *c.* 1930s, is Wintis White, a forest laborer who replaced Mr. Denegal upon his retirement as the forest foreman. (Courtesy of Joe Spaulding Jr.)

Contractors were engaged for extensive construction projects such as the installation of sewers and the additions to the clubhouse. Above, men, probably employed by a contractor, shovel ditches for a water pipeline. (JIM.)

106

A dairy, probably built because of delivery and consistency problems with cream and butter orders, supplied dairy products, as well as eggs to the clubhouse and cottage owners. Staffed by a dairyman, the main section of the building was used to milk cows and the smaller part for churning butter. The silo stored feed for the cows. When the farm closed in 1930, dairy products were purchased from local businesses, such as the Butler Island Dairy. (JIM.)

Besides cleaning the clubhouse linens and towels, the laundry, seen above, c. 1903, took care of the members' washables. While many of the cottages had laundry rooms, some of the owners chose to use the club laundry. Members were charged per article laundered, and, in 1908 or 1909, a shirt was cleaned and pressed for 12¢ and a dress from 40¢ to $3. Until the mid-1930s, the laundry took care of employees' clothing free of charge. (JIM.)

In 1925, the club hired a head laundress, a washer, a bundlewasher, a starcher, two Mangle operators (a machine used for pressing), an ironer, a fancy ironer, a shirt ironer, as well as two helpers and a fireman to work in the laundry. Above, c. 1903, an employee hangs clothes up to dry. Below, c. 1928–29, laundry workers have their picture taken beside the laundry building. (both JIM.)

Above, c. 1914, the club carpenter, Chris Nielsen, and his wife, Nikoline, relax on the porch of an employee house they used from 1912–22. By the 1930s, 28 employee homes were located on the island. Mr. Nielsen, besides repairing and maintaining club structures, replanked the *Jekyl Island* steamer, rebuilt the *Kitty* launch, and constructed the *Sylvia* launch. (JIM.)

In 1929, Oswald Curet, earning $160 a month, was the club carpenter. His wife, seen right, was a devoted animal lover. During her husband's employment, Mrs. Curet fostered two deer, reputedly tame enough to sleep by her bed, and cared for raccoons, which often frolicked in a hanging basket on the Curet's employee house porch. Other carpenters employed by the club included Chips Torkelson, George Cowman Jr., and R. Arcott. By the 1920s, Tom Parland, a nephew of Page Parland, assisted the carpenter. (JIM.)

Although the club employed a carpenter, most of the island structures were built by private contractors who used crews to quickly complete construction projects. Above, c. 1918, George Cowman Sr., a contractor, sits on the commissary steps, a building he erected in 1916. The commissary was staffed by a clerk, earning $75 a month in 1925. During the 1930s, the employee store closed, and Sim Denegal's off-season commissary in the Quarters was used year-round. (JIM.)

George Cowman Sr.'s work crew pauses for a break during construction of the James Memorial Wall, a monument honoring Dr. Walter James's contributions as president of the club. Standing far left, c. 1930, Cecil Grantham Sr. was the foreman of Mr. Cowman's employees. (JIM.)

Holding up a zigzag ruler, club carpenter Chris Nielsen kneels behind, and the men in front from left to right are: Don Cameron, John Sharp, and his brother-in-law, Axel Lindstrom, c. 1914. Mr. Cameron, as well as Mr. Sharp, worked in the garage, chauffeuring during the day and washing cars in the evening. With automobiles responsible for phasing out horse and carriages, chauffeurs and mechanics replaced liveried drivers and stablemen on the club payroll. By the 1910s, the club's stable was converted into a garage. (JIM.)

Above, c. 1910s, a group of workers and their spouses rest on the boarding house steps. The boarding house was home for the club truck driver, the plumbers, the chauffeurs, temporary craftsmen, such as contractor work crews and other employees. Meals were prepared and served for the residents by a cook and waitress. Above, two chauffeurs sit in the front row beside two unidentified women. In the back row, from left to right, are: child Howard Etter, Chief Electrical Engineer Gilbert Kay, Axel Lindstrom, Ray Etter, and Mrs. Kay. (JIM.)

The building of a power plant in 1902 changed the club's interior illumination from kerosene lamps and coal gas fixtures to electric lights. The generating equipment, purchased from the General Electric Company, was operated in 1925 by a chief electrical engineer, an electrician, two engineers, and two firemen. This picture is dated c. 1903. (JIM.)

A watertank, located in the clubhouse attic, was so heavy that its weight was damaging the floors and walls of the clubhouse. To remedy this problem, a water tower was built in 1892, seen here c. 1903, with a windmill pumping artesian water into the storage tank. Eventually, other towers, using electrical pumps, were erected within the enclosure. (JIM.)

Myrtle Lindsey (standing right), *c.* 1932, was employed as the club's beautician. Ms. Lindsey did not receive a salary, instead she retained the earnings from her services, which included cutting hair, giving manicures, and performing facials. Unlike the club barber, who operated a one-chair shop in the clubhouse basement, the beautician traveled to the clubhouse rooms and cottages to work. Dick Harvey, possibly standing center, was the "Red Bug" repairman, earning $60 a month in 1932. (JIM.)

Staffed by an employee earning $100 a month in 1925, the bicycle shop was used as a repair and storage facility for the club-owned bikes. During times when the club purchased new bicycles, the old ones were sold to year-round workers. Above, *c.* 1910s, Nikoline Nielsen and her brother, Axel Lindstrom, stand on the bicycle shop ramp. Mr. Lindstrom assisted Chris Nielsen, the club carpenter, in the construction of the *Sylvia* launch. (JIM.)

This picture is dated c. 1890s. Working in a one-room structure near the upholstery shop, the taxidermist stuffed and mounted animals and birds into a realistic pose. In the early years, the taxidermist was in constant demand, however, as hunting waned, the need for this service diminished. (JIM.)

In the early 1900s, tree trunks around the gamekeepers home, seen partially above, c. 1903, were whitewashed using lime. Whitewashing of trees, thought to be aesthetically pleasing, was also done within the enclosure on trees around the Quarters. The gamekeeper was hired to help increase island wildlife as well as care for the hunting dogs. Initially, three employee houses, adjacent to the dairy, were used by the gamekeeper, assistant gamekeeper, and the dairyman. (JIM.)

Hired in 1910, Karl Keffer (second from right), c. 1910s, was the club's golf professional for 32 years. During the summer, he worked as the professional for the Royal Ottawa Golf Club, but, by winter, he returned to the island and resided in an employee house constructed specifically for him and his wife, Isabella. Mr. Keffer, earning $50 a month in 1925, often had other golf professionals assisting him. John Etter (standing far left) was the brother-in-law of Don Cameron (second from left). Axel Lindstrom stands at the far right. (JIM.)

Teenagers were hired to work during the season as caddies, and, by the 1920s, around 20 young men toted golf bags by day and attended school at night. The school for caddies was located in the center room of the U-shaped Caddy Lodge, a bunkhouse built in 1930 where meals were also served. Attached to one end of the Caddy Lodge was the caddy master's home. Willie Burroughs was employed for many years as the caddy master while his wife, Lottie, worked as the Caddy Lodge housekeeper. This picture is dated c. 1941. (Courtesy of the *Saturday Evening Post*.)

Members were often accompanied by personal employees, such as secretaries, governesses, nursemaids, and valets. Cottage owners included in their staff chambermaids, cooks, and laundry attendants. Above, c. 1910s, from left to right, are Anna; Lena Eickholz, a chambermaid; and Mrs. Payne, a cook, who all worked for the Albright family. Below, c. 1920s, pushing Frank and Dorothy Goodyear in a stroller, Hannah May Kelley (standing right) was employed for years as the Goodyear nursemaid. (both JIM.)

In the early years, many of the members shipped horses and carriages to the island. Personal stablemen and liveried drivers were hired to attend the animals and rigs. Pomeroy, seen above, worked at least one season as a carriage driver for the Maurice family. (JIM.)

The first car was brought to the island in 1901 by William Struthers. He was asked to remove it. Later that year, cars were allowed but with certain restrictions. By the 1910s, automobiles became the primary source of transportation, shipped over by members. Pictured to the right is an unidentified member's chauffeur sitting on the hood of a car. For a fee, car problems could be taken care of in the club garage. The charge for using the club's mechanic in 1942, not including parts, was $1.50 an hour. (JIM.)

Cottage owners had the option of using the club's groundskeeping staff to care for their lawns; however, many chose to hire caretakers. Charlie Hill, seen left, was employed on the island for 51 years, most of that time as the Maurice family caretaker. (JIM.)

Charlie Hill (standing center) began working as a club employee in 1891, but, shortly thereafter, he was hired as the Maurice family coachman. This position eventually turned into the cottage caretaker, in which he performed duties such as running errands, repairing broken items, and tending to the lawn. The Maurices constructed a home near their cottage for the Hill family, which included Mr. Hill's wife, Angie (right) and their daughter, Anna (left). (JIM.)

Edwin Gould hired Page Parland (above right) to be the family's caretaker, a position which included maintaining the lawns of Chicota cottage, Shrady cottage, and the Gould's Playhouse. Later, Mr. Parland also worked in the same capacity for Frank Gould as well as for Dr. Walter James. His wife, Aleathia (above left), was employed by several of the members to air out their cottages during the summer, which meant at least once a month opening windows for fresh air to circulate inside the homes. Below, the Goulds constructed a house for the Parland's use near their property. (both JIM.)

With so many married workers living on the island, it stands to reason that numerous children were raised on Jekyll. Above, c. 1910s, two teenagers, possibly nephews of Charlie Hill, pose along the side of Hollybourne cottage. Below, c. 1916, two children, one of which is the daughter of building contractor Thomas Gage, take a ride on the club's Ford truck. (both JIM.)

A schoolhouse, seen above, was constructed in the early 1900s for children of white employees. By the 1910s, it closed for lack of a substantial number of students. A strong storm reputedly destroyed the structure in 1915. By the 1930s, the commissary building was used as the schoolhouse. School teachers employed over the club period included Bertha Baker, F.L. Busheam, Della Willey, and Janie Goins. (JIM.)

Bertha Baker, standing far left, c. 1907, earned $17.50 a month in 1908 as the school teacher. Supposedly, Mrs. Frederic Baker, a club member and no relation to the teacher, matched her salary by an equal amount. Above, the children of Capt. James and Minnie Clark, George and Nellie Burbank, Chips and Lizzie Torkilson, and J. Henry and Tedia Thompson assemble near the schoolhouse. Mr. Burbank was the nightwatchman, hired to patrol the club enclosure. Mr. Thompson was the south end fisherman and guard, employed to protect oyster beds from poachers and procure seafood for members. (JIM.)

In the early years, many of the black employees as well as their children attended a summer school sponsored by the club. By the 1920s, a Red Row home, seen above, c. 1910s, was converted into a schoolhouse. Teachers employed for the school included Professor Wilder, Katye Cash, and Anna Hill. (JIM.)

The school teacher, Anna Hill (second row, far right), stands with her pupils near the schoolhouse porch. Ms. Hill, the daughter of Charlie Hill, earned $50 a month as the teacher in 1936. Included in the group of students are some of the children of William and Rosa Heck. Mr. Heck was an employee on the golf course. (JIM)

Above, *c.* 1910s, several of James and Margeret McDowell's children pose with other students for a class portrait. Mr. McDowell worked for years as the north end fisherman and guard. The position included the use of an employee house erected near the northwest side of the island. Another home was located on the opposite extremity for the south end fisherman and guard. (JIM.)

Employees' children play in front of Chicota cottage, *c.* early 1900s. The girl running towards the cottage is probably Catherine Clark, the daughter of Capt. James and Minnie Clark. Her brother Fred is possibly the child watching two boys carousing. (JIM.)

Above, c. 1910s, Howard Etter sits in the driver's seat while his brother, John Marshall, attempts to crank start the car. Their father was John Etter, the assistant superintendent. Below, c. early 1920s, from left to right, Clark Flanders, John Marshall Etter, Howard Etter, and David Nielsen pause from a bicycle ride near the Club Cottage. A first cousin to the Etter children, Clark Flanders's father, Hugh Flanders, was employed in the 1910s as the club mechanic. David Nielsen's father, Chris Nielsen, was the club carpenter during the 1910s and early 1920s. (JIM.)

Alfonzo Stafford, pictured at right c. 1936, stands on a step in front of a Red Row house used by his family. His father, Fred Stafford, was employed as a truck driver and a laborer for the club. The small dog, seen to the left of the door, was a french poodle given by the Goodyear family to Myer Hill's son Ray. The dog, named Frenchy, was secretly buried after its death in the club members' pet cemetery. The pet cemetery, located in an open field near the Brown cottage, had seven or eight pets buried there, including a parrot owned by Dr. Walter James and a cat owned by Walter Jennings. (JIM.)

An unidentified woman and children wait at the wharf for the club boat's departure to the mainland. Thomas and Kayte Cash's daughter Elaine stands front row, far left. Mr. Cash was a nephew of Sim Denegal. The windowed room in the background was a waiting area for club members and guests. (JIM.)

Joe Spaulding Jr., the son of Capt. Joe Spaulding, holds up the tail of a dolphin found dead in a fisherman's net, c. 1936. Joe Jr. often played a "hide and go seek" game in which tinfoil cigarette liners were formed into a ball and hidden for children to find. (Courtesy of Joe Spaulding Jr.)

Rufus Bennett's granddaughter Martha and the nephew of Ralph Henderson cling to the fingers of Ophelia Polite, c. 1940s. Mrs. Polite and her husband, Winslow "Pipsie" Polite, were employed for years as the caretakers for the White Servants Annex. Mr. Bennett was the island caretaker during WW II, and Mr. Henderson, during the same time period, was the nightwatchman. (Courtesy of Lillian Schaitberger.)

BIBLIOGRAPHY

Chernow, Ron. *The House of Morgan, an American Banking Dynasty and the Rise of Modern Finance*. New York: Simon & Schuster, 1990.

Cleveland, Harold van B., and Thomas F. Huertas. *Citibank 1812–1970*. Massachusetts: Harvard University Press, 1985.

Dictionary of American Biography. 20 volumes. New York: Charles Scribner's Sons, 1928-36.

Forbes, B.C. *Men Who Are Making America*. New York: B.C. Forbes Publishing Co., 1916–1917.

The Jekyll Island Museum Archives. The Jekyll Island Museum Archives. Jekyll Island, GA.

Lamont, Thomas. *Henry P. Davison: The Record of a Useful Life*. New York: Harper & Brothers Publishers, 1933.

Logan, Sheridan A. *George F. Baker and His Bank 1840-1955*. Stinehour Press and the Meriden Gravure Company, 1981.

McCash, William Bartron and June Hall McCash. *The Jekyll Island Club, Southern Haven for America's Millionaires*. Athens: The University of Georgia Press, 1989.

Martin, Harold H. *This Happy Isle, The Story of Sea Island and the Cloister*. Sea Island Company, 1978.

Morgan Papers. The J.P. Morgan Jr. Papers. The Pierpont Morgan Library. New York, N.Y.

National Cyclopedia of American Biography. numbered volumes. New Jersey: James T. White and Company, 1984.

Robinson, Lawrence. *History of The Blind Brook Club*. Privately printed, date unknown.

INTERVIEWS 1997–1998

Katheryn Etter Brown, Marjory Lederer Cardi, Katye Cash, Bill Cowman, Jane Ingalls Davidson, Martha Diaz, Whitney Ellsworth, Howard Ernest Etter, Hugh Clark Flanders, Roberta From, Robert Gardner Jr., Dr. Ray Hill, Sheridan Logan, Myrtle Lindsey Lyons, David Nielsen, A.J. Drexel Paul Jr., Carrie Maxwell Robinson, James Stillman Rockefeller, Lillian Schaitberger, Anita Souter, Joe Spaulding Jr., Dorethea Mitchell Stafford, Eugenia Stallman, Sam Snead, and J. Wesley Wellman.

ACKNOWLEDGMENTS

Thanks is due to my parents, Charles and Susan, for their encouragement, help, and support. This book would not have been possible without the numerous people, past and present, who have diligently gathered and preserved the history of the Jekyll Island Club. In particular, I would like to single out Bart and June McCash. My sincere gratitude goes to David Stough for setting this project in motion. Also, my appreciation extends to Warren Murphey and the rest of the museum staff, including Leslie Hicks, Karen Mcinnis, Pam Herrin, Vicki Wildes, and all of the historical interpreters. I am indebted to Wesley Wellman, who spent hours of his time retracing the club enclosure, studying photographs, and enlightening me with his knowledge of the club as well as of numerous other subjects. I would like to give special recognition to Myrtle Lindsey Lyons, David Nielsen, Lillian Schaitberger and Martha Diaz, and Joe Spaulding Jr. for taking time to actually visit me on Jekyll Island to share their stories. Thank you! I am also grateful to the following persons, organizations, and companies for their assistance and/or contributions: John Baird, Lawrence Baker Jr., Bob Battaly and the Rockefeller Archive Center, The Blind Brook Club, Katheryn Etter Brown, Marjory Lederer Card, Katye Cash, Bill Cowman, Leigh Creech, Jane Ingalls Davidson, Barbara Davis, Christa McDowell Davis, Whitney Ellsworth, Howard Ernest Etter, Rose Fields, Hugh Clark Flanders, Roberta From, Robert Gardner Jr., Robert Haase and Glynn Camera, Wes Haynes, Howard Kinney, Sheridan Logan, Mrs. J. Couper Lord Jr., June McCash, James Maloney and the Pulitzer Publishing Company, Christine Nelson and the Pierpont Morgan Library, A.J. Drexel Paul Jr., Johnny Paulk, Steve Pettinga and the *Saturday Evening Post*, Cherry McDowell Pittman, Mary Plyer, Sharon Proudfoot and the Sea Island Company, Carrie Maxwell Robinson, James Stillman Rockefeller, Howard Sapp, Martha McDowell Scoggin, Anita Souter, Dorethea Mitchell Stafford, Eugenia Stallman, Sam Snead, Wayne Tindall, and Bob Wyllie and the Coastal Georgia Historical Society. Finally, appreciation goes to Jim Dunn for his assistance and patience.